TRANSMITTAL LETTER

MAY 5, 2015

The United States Advisory Commission on Public Diplomacy (ACPD), authorized pursuant to Public Law 112-239 [Sec.] 1280(a)-(c), hereby submits this white paper, "Public Diplomacy At Risk: Protecting Open Access for American Centers." ACPD is a bipartisan panel created by Congress in 1948 to formulate and recommend policies and programs to carry out the public diplomacy functions vested in U.S. government entities and to appraise the effectiveness of those activities. It was reauthorized in January 2013 to complete the Comprehensive Annual Report on Public Diplomacy and International Broadcasting Activities, and to produce other reports and white papers that support effective public diplomacy.

This white paper is a follow up to the 1985 ACPD report, "Terrorism and Security: The Challenge for Public Diplomacy," which was submitted in reaction to the Inman Standards and their possible effect on the U.S. Information Agency (USIA). Today, ACPD is concerned about the pending shuttering of 21 American Centers. These Centers are essential platforms for core public diplomacy activities, such as alumni engagement, education advising for U.S. universities, English-language education, cultural programming, and speakers and forums on U.S. policy issues. They are also located in cities that are becoming increasingly important incubators for empowerment and are home to highly networked societies, such as Jerusalem; Beijing and Shanghai; Mexico City; and New Delhi.

We greatly admire the tenacity and the talent of our public diplomats, who sometimes work in high-risk, high-threat environments to engage foreign publics in the advancement of U.S. foreign policy. We are also grateful to the many State Department officials who helped us uncover data for this report.

Respectfully Submitted,

William J. Hybl, Chair
(Colorado)

Sim Farar, Vice Chair
(California)

Lyndon L. Olson, Vice Chair
(Texas)

Penne Korth Peacock
(Texas)

Anne Wedner
(Illinois)

Lezlee J. Westine
(Virginia)

EXECUTIVE SUMMARY

American Spaces – overseas physical platforms to inform and engage foreign audiences -- provide a fundamental foundation for U.S. public diplomacy efforts. The U.S. Advisory Commission on Public Diplomacy deeply understands how difficult it is to balance the need for security with the mission of foreign public engagement, especially in high-risk, high-threat environments. The hardening of our posts through the Secure Embassy Construction and Counterterrorism Act of 1999 (SECCA) was a logical and pragmatic response to a host of devastating attacks against U.S. embassy spaces in the 1980s and 1990s. Yet it is imperative that we reconsider how the relocation of free-standing American Centers to U.S. embassy, consulate and annex compounds can complicate the essential goals of public diplomacy to understand, inform and engage foreign audiences to advance U.S. foreign policy. Once the American Centers move to these compounds, they transform into less accessible Information Resource Centers (IRCs) that attract six times fewer visitors than American Centers.

There are currently 715 American Spaces worldwide. Of them, just 17 percent are U.S.-controlled spaces: American Centers (32) and Information Resource Centers (87). The remaining 83 percent are partner spaces: Binational Centers (117) and American Corners (479). The preferred American Space is the stand-alone American Center, which is publicly available in urban centers abroad and allows for a broad range of public diplomacy programming, such as EducationUSA advising, cultural programs, and forums on U.S. foreign policy issues.

In the past 10 years, eight of these centers have moved from urban centers to secure compounds, downsizing into IRCs that have stricter security regulations for foreign citizens. In the next 10 years, we understand that 21 of the remaining 32 American Centers are facing possible relocation due to the construction of new embassy, consular, and annex compounds. While U.S. public diplomacy officers worldwide often reach target audiences through partner spaces such as American Corners and Binational Centers, the success of these spaces hinges on the willingness of host institutions to work with the U.S. government, in addition to other variables outside of the officers' control.

ACPD believes that the construction and security maintenance of U.S. facilities must consider the mission goals and objectives, of which engagement with publics is often vital. We are concerned that SECCA may be automatically and asymmetrically applied to U.S.-controlled public diplomacy platforms, American Centers and IRCs, regardless of the characteristics of individual cases. This is an issue that has been of concern to ACPD since 1985, when the Inman Standards were first introduced after the attacks against the U.S. mission in Lebanon.[1] Since the enactment of SECCA in 1999, the shuttering of American Centers and closed access of IRCs has been raised by the Senate Foreign Relations Committee and the Government Accountability Office. Today, we are worried that the closing of American Centers is accelerating and emphasize the need for selective and flexible application, on a case-by-case basis, of security standards.

Of course, in extreme cases where an evaluation by the State Department and the embassy determines that the threat landscape cannot support a public diplomacy space, closing centers must be considered. But to keep American Centers standing and IRCs open and accessible, wherever possible, ACPD makes four core recommendations:

- **Congress: Enact a "Sense of Congress" to Keep American Centers Open and IRCs Accessible.** The presumption that public diplomacy platforms should automatically be co-located within compounds, based on SECCA, should be reversed.[2] We advise the creation of a "Sense of the Congress" in future State Department Authorization bills that clearly indicate that the Secretary of

State should give favorable consideration to requests for American Centers to remain in urban locations and exercise his/her waiver authority under section 606(a)(2)(B) of the Secure Embassy Construction and Counterterrorism Act of 1999 (22 U.S.C. 4865(a)(2)(B)) in order to permit American Centers to remain separate from U.S. embassies abroad and ensure that IRCs on U.S. embassy, consulate and annex compounds remain open and accessible.[3] This would help to simplify co-location waiver requests at the State Department and emphasize the need for a flexible, case by case approach that takes into consideration the centrality of public diplomacy to fulfilling U.S. missions.[4]

- **State Department: Aim to Make Existing IRCs Open and Accessible Through New Policy.** IRCs, especially in countries that are pivotal to U.S. national security, must become more engaging to attract audiences. A worldwide policy for open access to IRCs that applies to all posts is necessary. This would lift "by appointment only" restrictions where they exist; create a separate security screening from the main chancery; permit unescorted access; and allow use of personal electronic devices and wireless internet access. Wherever possible, U.S. employees should have offices in the IRCs so they can regularly interact with visitors. American Centers that transform into IRCs should particularly adhere to these principles to retain relationships and networks.

- **State Department: Conduct a Study of the Impact of American Centers, IRCs, Binational Centers and American Corners.** As a result of the 2010 Government Accountability Office (GAO) report on American Spaces, the State Department has conducted two major studies that have supported the improved management of these Spaces: a 2014 study on the user experience of American Centers and a 2015 study on the value of "by appointment only" IRCs. We also recommend a third study on the impact and value of these spaces -- American Centers, IRCs, Binational Centers and American Corners -- for U.S. foreign policy goals, especially in the IIP-determined "top tier" spaces. The appraisals should link their efforts to mission goals and develop a research-based strategic plan for each space, identifying key publics and the public diplomacy impact objectives for each key public.[5]

- **State Department: Continue Dialogue Between Public Diplomacy, Bureau of Overseas Building Operations and the Bureau of Diplomatic Security Leadership.** We are encouraged that Diplomatic Security and the Overseas Building Operations Bureaus have already created a working group with public diplomacy leadership to address several policy, planning and funding concerns with the remaining free-standing American Centers and the IRCs. We hope that these conversations will continue to be constructive and tackle the accessibility of these spaces on a case-by-case basis.

INTRODUCTION

American Spaces – overseas physical platforms to inform and engage foreign audiences -- provide a fundamental foundation for U.S. public diplomacy efforts. For nearly a century, they have been official platforms designed to connect the United States with the host country and to expand the cultural and social ties between both countries. The spaces encourage two-way flows of information and help the U.S. to create and maintain relationships with a cross-section of society, including the media, academics, writers, students, activists, cultural figures, youth, and representatives of minority and women's groups. In short, they are platforms for U.S. officials to convene networks vital to our national security and our broader foreign policy goals.

The Secure Embassy Construction and Counterterrorism Act of 1999 (SECCA), which mandated the creation of New Embassy Compounds (NECs), New Consular Compounds (NCCs) and New Annex Compounds (NOXs), has had a profound effect on the openness and accessibility of American Centers and Information Resource Centers (IRCs) that are housed in U.S. government-owned and -leased facilities. SECCA requires all U.S. agencies in country be co-located on the compounds and that there be a 100-foot setback from the perimeter at each newly acquired facility.[6]

Of the current 715 American Spaces worldwide, just 17 percent are U.S.-controlled spaces: American Centers (32) and Information Resource Centers (87). The remaining 83 percent of them are partner spaces: Binational Centers (117) and American Corners (479).[7]

Information Resource Centers (IRCs) are libraries with some space for public outreach activities. They often operate in cramped, restrictive spaces that are located in hard-to-reach locations. Currently 87 IRCs are open to the public. An additional 37 are "by appointment only," requiring a 24-hour or 48-hour lead time before members of the public can access the space. Since 2004,

61 Information Resource Centers worldwide have been shuttered due to various reasons, although some still operate as management centers for American Spaces within Public Affairs Sections.

U.S. partner spaces (Binational Centers and American Corners) have been important alternatives to American Centers and IRCs, offering open access and binational programming. Yet they hinge on the reliability of host partners and the willingness of a host institution to publically associate themselves with U.S. foreign policy goals.

The preferred American Space is the stand-alone American Center, which is accessible to publics and allows for a broad range of public diplomacy programming, such as Education USA advising, cultural programs, and forums on U.S. foreign policy issues. Visitors to an American Center may come for one activity, such as educational advising, and then stay for others, such as a panel discussion on an important issue for the mission.

In the past 10 years, eight American Centers – including ones in Bucharest, Guangzhou, Mumbai and Riga -- have moved from their urban locations to secure facilities, transforming into IRCs. With SECCA co-location requirements, there is continuing pressure to transform American Centers into IRCs. In the next 10 years, ACPD understands that 21 American Centers are facing co-location, which could lead to an absence of U.S. public outreach in such urban power centers as Jerusalem, Mexico City, New Delhi and Shanghai. As we previously wrote in our paper with the Atlantic Council on globalization and public diplomacy, "Diplomacy for a Diffuse World," if the U.S. does not adapt policies and structures to increasing urbanization, we risk weakening our ability to fully understand and shape developments impacting U.S. national security and the international system.[60]

DEFINITIONS OF AMERICAN SPACES

American Spaces[25] are physical platforms designed to engage with people who may never travel to the U.S., but can use the space to learn about American culture, society and foreign policy. The Office of the Inspector General has emphasized that the spaces are preferable to digital platforms, as they allow diplomats to inform and engage foreign publics "in a more hands-on approach ... [which] can help build mean-ingful personal relationships upon which future foreign policy relationships can be formed, and thus assist in accomplishing long term policy objectives."[26] There are 715 American Spaces in 153 countries. Among them are U.S.-controlled spaces, 32 American Centers (4%) and 87 Information Resource Centers (12%); and partner spaces, 117 Binational Centers (16%) and 479 American Corners (67%).[27]

	AF	EAP	EUR	NEA	SCA	WHA	TOTAL
American Center	7	12	3	5	4	1	32
IRCs	13	13	19	5	6	12	87
American Corner	98	61	159	44	86	31	479
Binational Center	0	0	10	0	0	107	117
TOTAL	137	86	191	54	96	151	715

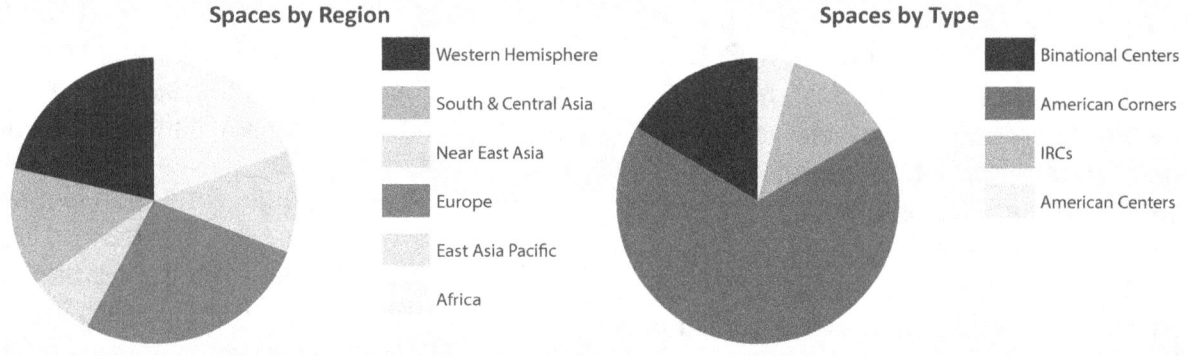

Spaces by Region

- Western Hemisphere
- South & Central Asia
- Near East Asia
- Europe
- East Asia Pacific
- Africa

Spaces by Type

- Binational Centers
- American Corners
- IRCs
- American Centers

U.S.-CONTROLLED SPACES

American Centers are stand-alone, U.S. government-owned or -leased facilities located outside of the main U.S. chancery or consulate's building that are accessible to the public. They are staffed by U.S. embassy employees or U.S. government-funded contract staff and are under the direction of the Public Affairs Officer. The Centers typically house a library, in addition to a broad range of public diplomacy activities such as EducationUSA advising, cultural programs, speakers and forums on U.S. foreign policy, in addition to providing open Internet access and video-conferences. Visitors to an American Center may come for one activity, such as educational advising, and then stay for others, such as panel discussions or featured speakers on policy issues.

Information Resource Centers are smaller than American Centers and normally placed within U.S. embassy, consulate or annex compounds. The IRCs provide information services to the public, including access to the Internet, and to U.S. Embassy staff. They can also be a platform for cultural or speakers programs. In addition, some provide EducationUSA advising. In countries where there are Binational centers or American Corners, IRCs provide an administrative link between the embassy and the network of American Spaces.

Note: 87 are open to the public with set hours, 37 are "by appointment only", and 61 are closed. The State Department is currently conducting a review of by appointment-only IRCs to determine which are meeting operating standards, and which should be closed. For the purpose of this paper, we are only counting the 87 that are open to the public with set hours.

PARTNER SPACES

Binational Centers are private, autonomous, non-profit institutions that are autonomous, self-sustaining organizations, created through agreements between the host government and the United States. They normally focus on providing En-glish-language education for a fee, which makes them self-financed. The 117 BNCs are mostly concentrated in major cities in 18 countries in Central America, South America, and the Caribbean. Ten of them are located in Europe. They can support educational advising for study in the U.S., serve as network centers for USG alumni, house libraries with information on the U.S., and provide space for U.S. cultural programming.

American Corners are collections of American materials and programming spaces within a local host institution, such as a library or university, which provides information about the United States via books, magazines, and multi-media sources, including access to research databases and the Internet. They are staffed and managed by the host institution. American Corners operate in locations where budget and security constraints have made full information centers unfeasible and where the public can often not access IRCs. In some locations, they can provide advising for study in the U.S. and cultural programming.

BACKGROUND

The issue of balancing the accessibility of American Spaces with security needs was first articulated in the U.S. Advisory Commission on Public Diplomacy's 1985 report, "Terrorism and Security: The Threat to Public Diplomacy."[8] Today, ACPD is grappling with the same dilemma as it did 30 years ago: How does the United States conduct public diplomacy abroad and, at the same time, protect the security of its personnel and facilities?

The 1983 attacks on the U.S. Embassy and Marine barracks in Beirut, which killed 17 American civilians and 241 Marines, as well as the attack on the U.S. Embassy in Kuwait, which killed no Americans, devastated the diplomatic communi-ty and led to a review of the State Department's security posture. The Advisory Panel on Overseas Security at the State Department, or the "Inman Panel" (as it was known in honor of its Chairman, Admiral Bobby Ray Inman) created the Bureau of Diplomatic Security and proposed the Inman Standards, which stated that all embassies should be set back at least 100 feet from the street and be located on plots of 15 acres or more, and preferably outside of city centers. It was also recommended that U.S. Information Agency (USIA) libraries also relocate from city centers to the fortified embassy compounds.[9]

ACPD, which supported the USIA at the time,

protested that the panel did not take into consideration the unique role that public diplomacy plays in statecraft and the need for libraries and other public platforms to remain accessible to foreign citizens. It emphasized that since threats can rapidly change and vary from country to country, and sometimes city to city, flexibility and understanding of the role public diplomacy plays in each mission is essential. In an October 1985 op-ed in the Washington Post, "Don't Let Security Hide Our Light," Edwin Fuelner, President of the Heritage Foundation and Chairman of the ACPD, wrote: "USIA's public affairs officers know that by retreating … the agency will become inaccessible to most of the people it is trying to reach … wholesale retreat to safe, but inaccessible, enclaves is not the answer. Personal contact with global opinion leaders is essential to the conduct of American foreign policy."[10]

The horrific terrorist attacks against the U.S. embassies in Nairobi and Dar es Salaam in 1998 led to the passing of the Secure Embassy Construction and Counterterrorism Act of 1999 (SECCA)[11], which institutionalized many of Inman Standards, including the requirement of the 100 foot setback of U.S. government facilities between the building exterior and perimeter of the property on which the facility is sited.[12] It required that all U.S. diplomatic facilities co-locate on the embassy, consulate or annex compound, including American Centers.[13] Section 606(a)(3) of SECCA however, required that Congress provide some flexibility in the statute by allowing the Secretary of State to waive the restrictions if s/he can certify that security considerations permit the waiver.

In 2003, Senator Richard Lugar, Chairman of the Committee on Foreign Relations at the U.S. Senate (SFRC), first raised the effect SECCA was having on foreign public engagement activities publicly. While questioning General Charles Williams, Director of the Office of Overseas Building Operations, and Ambassador Francis Taylor, Assistant Secretary of State for Diplomatic Security, at the March 2003 hearing, "Safer Embassies in Unsafe Places," he questioned how everyday people could know about U.S. public diplomacy

resources when they were behind barriers. He stated, "We are in the public diplomacy arena, and you may be doing better in security than we are doing in public diplomacy, although this is arguable. Both are very tough challenges, but nevertheless, they are both important, and trying to determine how to do these things simultaneously is a challenge."[61]

In 2009, Senator Lugar, under Senator John Kerry's Chairmanship, submitted the SFRC report, "U.S. Public Diplomacy – Time to Get Back in the Game," written by Professional Staff Member, Paul Foldi.[14] The report stated that by co-locating American Centers on new embassy, consulate and annex compounds, "we have created a vicious cycle: frustrated by our inability to connect with audiences overseas who no longer trust us, we have in fact weakened our efforts at Public Diplomacy by denying them access to both American officials as well as uncensored information about us."[15]

The report emphasized that the State Department, Congress and host governments should work together to re-create the American Center system in secure facilities outside U.S. embassy compounds from which U.S. officials can connect with foreign publics. Among the report's 12 recommendations was a call for SECCA's co-location requirement to be re-visited so that remaining American Centers can remain as free-standing, and new American Centers can be established off-compound as long as appropriate security measures are in place.[17]

The following year, the Government Accountability Office (GAO) found that one-third of the IRCs they examined on the secure compounds had insufficient space or were in an inaccessible location for the public. In many locations, IRC staff noted to GAO that security procedures restricted visitors and impeded their ability to conduct research about the United States.[18] The report read that security restrictions "portray U.S. embassies and consulates as unwelcoming places. Visitors to public diplomacy facilities may also be deterred by screening measures they must undergo prior to entry."[19] Concerns about fortress-like compounds and how they can repel publics from engaging with the U.S. have been echoed in several pieces of commentary, including from former U.S. Agency for International Development (US-AID) Administrator Andrew Natsios, who lamented, "It's hard to carry out our foreign policy from behind thick concrete walls."[20]

Recently, State Department leadership has recognized the need for greater risk tolerance to achieve U.S. foreign policy goals. On April 17, the Under Secretary for Management announced the publication of a new Risk Management Policy in the Foreign Affairs Manual (02 FAM 30), which emphasizes that "State Department employees and leaders must not simply avoid risk: they must proactively manage it in pursuit of U.S. foreign policy objectives."[23] The 2015 Quadrennial Diplomacy and Development Review (QDDR) stated on April 29 that the Secretary of State and other Department leaders will begin conversations with Congress and the American people about "the realities of risk in our work and the need for greater risk-tolerance" in addition to providing "leaders and employees with a consistent approach to making decisions in the face of challenging, fluid, and unclear circumstances, while recognizing that there are no one-size-fits–all solutions."[21] In addition, a new team of State Department offi-

cials, along with those from USAID, will "review past and current operations in dangerous environments" in order to "explore ways to streamline operations and increase flexibility in [those] environments."[22]

ACPD applauds these policy changes as they apply directly to how we approach public diplomacy. The need for this new direction intersects with findings from our 2014 qualitative research with more than 60 stakeholders on risk tolerance and management, in coordination with the U.S. Institute of Peace, the McCain Institute for International Leadership, and the Truman National Security Project/Center for National Policy. The consensus among civilians who conduct various diplomatic and development activities was that they are willing to take risks to achieve mission goals if they feel that reasonable precautions have been taken for their safety. In addition, the overwhelming majority of those interviewed stated that relying on digital tools to inform and influence foreign audiences does not sufficiently replace in-person engagement.[24] In this modern, digital era, American Centers remain essential physical platforms for U.S. officials to establish and maintain relationships with foreign citizens, and cultivate networks that can help to advance U.S. foreign policy goals.

AMERICAN CENTERS AT RISK

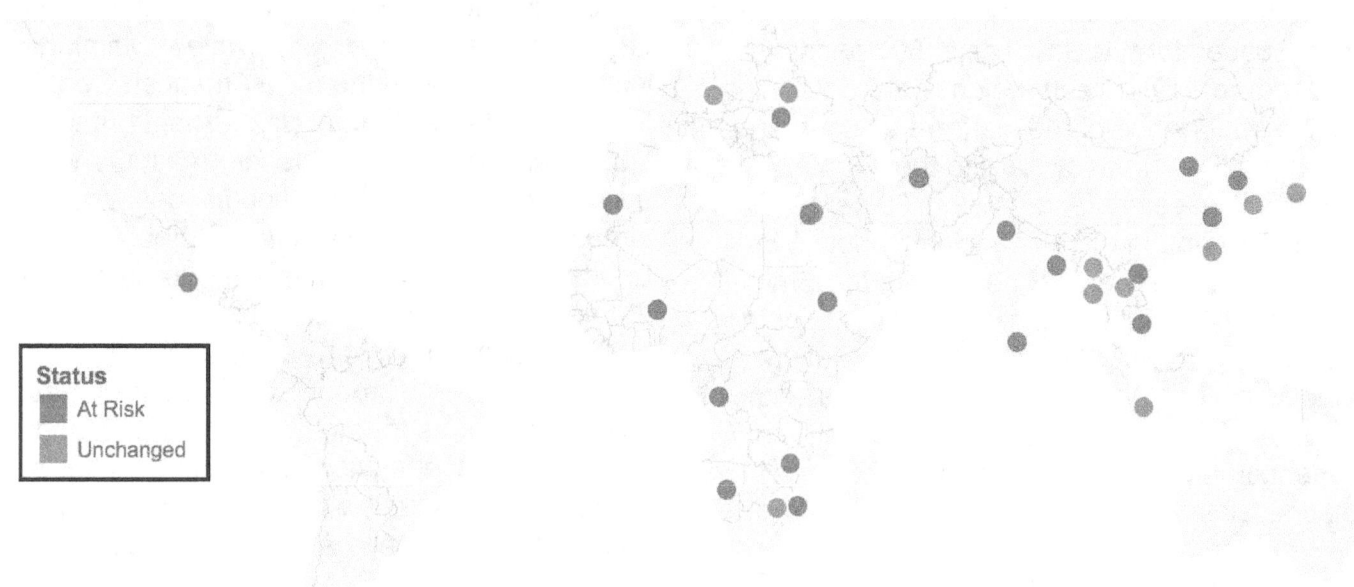

Status
At Risk
Unchanged

STRATEGIC IMPORTANCE OF AMERICAN SPACES

Open and accessible American Spaces provide a platform for U.S. officials to directly engage with average citizens abroad, many of whom have no contact with Americans. They provide room for five core public diplomacy activities in support of U.S. mission priorities: cultural programming and events; news and information about the U.S.; English language education oppotunities; student advising via EducationUSA; and recruitment and alumni engagement of U.S. exchange program participants.[28] Especially in places where the Internet is restricted, the spaces are meant to provide uncensored, open access with the best available broadband capacity.

The Bureau of International Information Programs (IIP) at the U.S. Department of State oversees worldwide American Spaces from Washington. Though IIP provides a majority of funding and resources for American Spaces in IIP, control over day-to-day management of the spaces is largely retained by the mission. In FY14, the Office of American Spaces operated with a $9 million budget. In addition, the office distributes roughly $15 million of funds to posts to modernize and maintain spaces that provide a high value public diplomacy experience. In order to determine the best allocation of these resources, IIP collaborated with regional policy experts to identify the most strategically important American Spaces for the U.S. These 60 spaces (see addendum), 10 in each region, were determined by the importance of the platform as compared to other public diplomacy tools in the country. These "top tier" spaces receive roughly 60 percent of the $15 million in extra financial support.[29] In some cases, IIP has partnered with the Smithsonian Institution to make maximum use of the space, showcasing American history, culture, innovation and policy. Some of these strategic spaces are American Corners if there are not American Centers in country, or if IRCs are in inaccessible locations.[30]

In a 2014 study of the user's experience of American Centers, 20 percent stated they intention-

ally went to a Center to engage and learn more about the U.S.[31] The remaining 80 percent were drawn to the spaces for their various resources, which signals that American Centers provide an entry point for the remaining 80 percent to learn about U.S. policy, society, culture and the various opportunities to travel to the United States. Below are some of the U.S. public diplomacy activities-that converge in American Spaces:

U.S. Education Advising: More than 840,000 international students come to study at U.S. higher education institutions each year on various visas. In 2013/14, these students contributed $27 billion to the American economy, according to the Department of Commerce.[32] To help facilitate this, there are 400 EducationUSA centers worldwide that support students in their applications to American colleges and universities. Twenty-five percent of EducationUSA advisors are located in American Spaces and another 25 percent in IRCs; 10 percent are located inside Fulbright Commissions; and 30 percent in local universities and libraries.[33] In 2014, the advisors made in-person contact with 3.6 million potential students worldwide through these spaces and an additional 3.6 million through virtual contact.[34]

Alumni Engagement: There are more than 1 million alumni of U.S. educational, cultural and professional exchanges worldwide.[35] Maintaining relationship with them via American Centers, IRCs and other American Spaces is a prime opportunity to communicate information and policies about the U.S. with audiences who are already familiar with the United States. The Educational and Cultural Affairs Bureau's (ECA) Alumni Affairs Division has supported more than 1,000 projects that involved more than 420,000 exchange alumni abroad.[36] The American Spaces offer platforms for the U.S. to maintain and strengthen these relationships, and to foster a network of individuals who have personal experience with the U.S. and American values.

English Language Education: Providing English-language education is a priority of U.S. public diplomacy efforts. American Spaces offer can provide English-language materials and a space for U.S. Regional English Language Officers (RELOs), English Language Fellows and Specialists, Massive Open Online Courses (MOOCs), and other courses provided by posts, to help students gain insight into U.S. culture and values, and an emphasis on active learning and critical thinking.

Other countries are equally aware of the importance of physical platforms to promote their culture and language and to promote study and travel to – and share information and news about -- their nations. European foreign cultural organizations such as the Alliance Française, British Council, and Goethe Institut operate independently of their respective embassies; China's Confucius Institutes are administered institutions affiliated with the Chinese Ministry of Education, including more than 95 housed in American universities.

China: Confucius Institutes -- More than 480

SECURITY AND AMERICAN SPACES

In 2014, a total of 31.7 million people visited the 715 American Spaces worldwide.[43] With the exception of the 117 Binational Centers (BNCs) in the Western Hemisphere Region and Europe, foreign institutions independent of the U.S. government, most foreign citizens visited the standalone 32 American Centers. Those Centers received nearly six times the amount of visitors compared to 87 IRC's (plus 37 "by appointment only" IRCs) located on these compounds.[44]

The closing and relocation of American Centers to new embassy, consular and annex compounds (NECs, NCCs, NOXs) severely diminishes their accessibility to foreign citizens.[45] Free-standing American Centers are located in urban centers, have reasonable yet consistent security for vis-

institutes operate worldwide to promote Chinese language and culture.[37]

Germany: Goethe Institut -- 159 institutes worldwide that promote the study of the German language abroad and encourage international cultural exchange and relations with Germany.[38]

France: Alliance Française -- 850 centers in 137 countries that promote French language and culture.[39]

UK: British Council -- 196 centers in 110 countries that promote English language instruction, British culture, arts and society, in addition to study in the UK; the centers provide a library and Internet locations. [40]

While the exact amount of them is unknown, Iran is also actively promoting Iranian Cultural Centers in Africa, Asia, the Middle East and the Western Hemisphere that offer Persian language classes, library resources, Iran studies programs, cultural programs, and religious events.[41] According to the SFRC 2009 report, the centers actively promote anti-American propaganda.[42]

itors and allow those visitors to maintain use of their cell phones and other electronic devices, while enjoying unescorted access. American Corners and Binational Centers also, depending on the host partner, can allow for largely unfettered access. IRCs, on the other hand, are normally located inside U.S. compounds situated outside of city centers, where public transportation is limited, and require restrictive security measures. In all but a few IRCs, visitors must temporarily surrender their mobile and other electronic devices, which means that those visitors cannot easily and digitally transfer information, take photos and/or share their experiences with others.[46] This discourages the casual visitor from engaging with the United States.

In addition, for the 37 IRCs that are "by appointment only," the need to schedule an appointment introduces a lag between initial visitor interest and actual access. Appointment times can vary from 24 to 48-hour advance notice. While the appointments help streamline security screening at the embassy, it deters the purpose of a public engagement platform.[47]

As mentioned, eight American Centers have shuttered since 2004.[48] In Fiscal Year 2012, the Office of American Spaces began to keep statistics on visitors to American Centers and IRCs. They found that program attendance dropped by 90 percent (from 24,062 to 2,331 people) after the Guangzhou American Center converted into an IRC. In India, when the Mumbai American Center, which had been open in the Churchgate district for more than 60 years, moved into the NCC that is remote from the city center and far from major transportation lines, the foot traffic dropped 57 percent (from 29,751 visitors in 2011 to 12,645 in 2012). The Public Affairs Section (PAS) in Mumbai conducted major efforts to tar-

VISITORS BY SPACE AND REGION

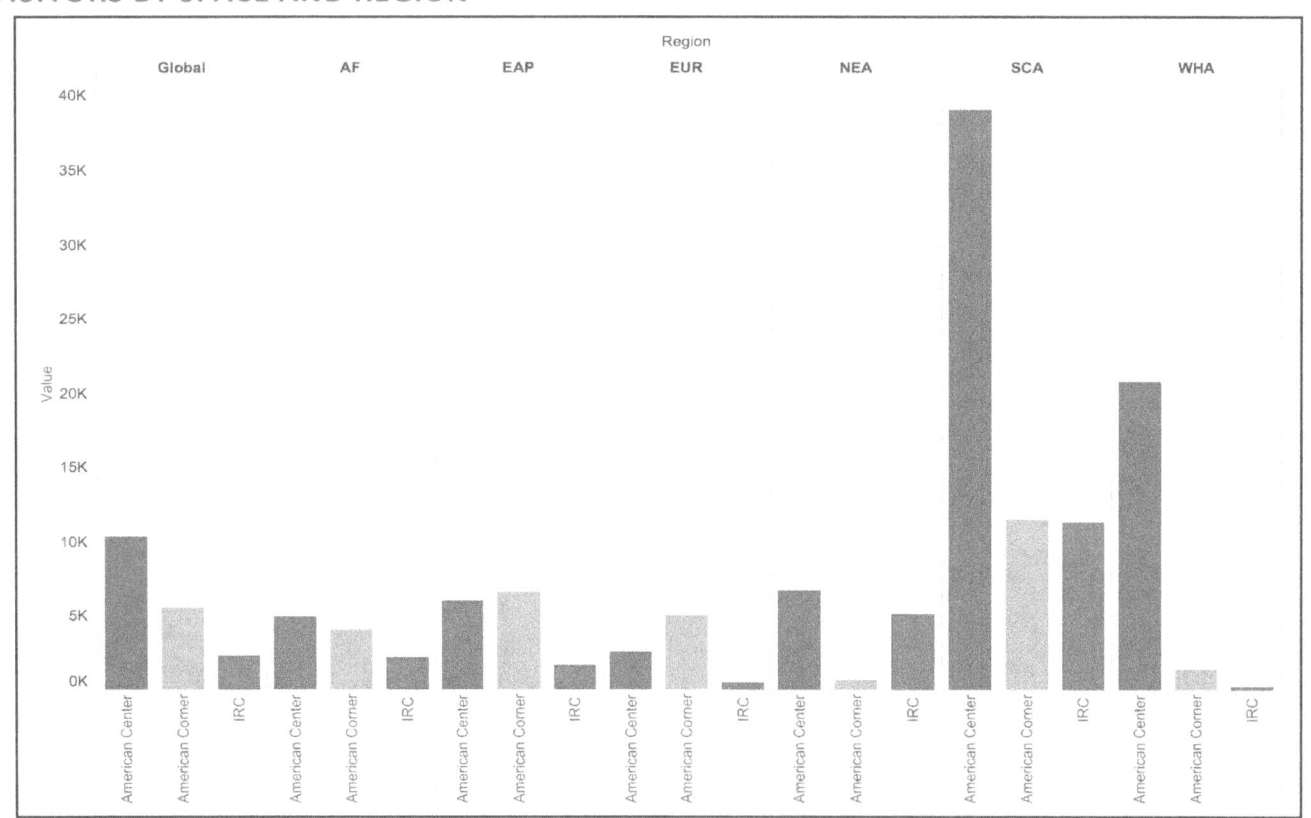

*BNCs excluded from chart. Though they have the highest participation they lack a global footprint comparable to other platforms.

get youth and, as a result, the Mumbai American Library has steadily increased its visitor rate. Yet it has never returned to the level it had previously enjoyed as a separate American Center. According to the PAS in Riga, Latvia, the transformation of its American Center in old town into an IRC in a remote location has brought foot traffic to a standstill. It is hoping to re-make the old chancery into a stand-alone American Center, which ACPD encourages given the particular need to engage Baltic publics in the face of Russian propaganda efforts.

Included in the 21 American Centers at risk for co-location the next 10 years are the Benjamin Franklin Library in Mexico City, which has been open since 1942 and is the only free-standing American Center in the Western Hemisphere;[49] the American Centers in Beijing and Shanghai; the American Centers in Jerusalem; and those in other cities of strategic importance for the U.S., like Chisinau, Moldova. Regardless of the threat level, American Centers' relocations to secure compounds can signal to local citizens that the U.S. does not have confidence in their country, or in them as a people.[50] As the SFRC report stated in 2009, "Where once [the U.S. was] seen as the world's leader in intellectual discourse and debate, we are now viewed as withdrawn and unconcerned with any views other than our own... If we hope to change opinions towards us, we must be able to interact with the world."[51] American Spaces have the fundamental purpose of building trust with local citizens. Shuttering American Centers and keeping IRCs inaccessible can isolate public diplomacy officers from their audiences and cripple their missions. Partner spaces have been important alternatives, yet the U.S. must rely on host partners and their openness to being associated with U.S. foreign policy goals. Finding credible partners can be especially difficult in places where bilateral relations are weak.

To maintain, and possibly expand, America's network of publicly accessible external platforms, the Secretary of State would have to waive the SECCA co-location requirement for American Centers. To ensure that IRCs are accessible and attractive to foreign citizens, leaders at post -- and those from the Public Diplomacy Cone, the Bureau of Overseas Buildings Operations and the Bureau of Diplomatic Security -- must meet regularly to discuss how to prioritize public diplomacy strategy in support of mission goals. Each American Center and IRC will present various challenges and opportunities to remain open and accessible. It will not make sense for every American Center worldwide to remain open and every IRC to become accessible and amenable to visitors' mobile technology. But it is vital that those discussions happen regularly and preferably at the outset of NEC/NCC/NOX construction.

CONCLUSION

Today's rapidly changing security environment requires constant collaboration between security and public diplomacy. Thirty years after ACPD first advocated keeping American Spaces open and accessible, we continue to grapple with the risks civilians often need to take to fulfill foreign policy missions. We agree with former ACPD Chair Ed Fuelner's 1985 statement that by retreating, public diplomacy officers can become inaccessible to the very publics that they are assigned to interact with, that wholesale withdrawal to enclaves is not the solution, and that regular contact with foreign publics is vital for U.S. foreign policy.[52] We are concerned that the trend of closing American Centers is quickly accelerating. We emphasize the need for selective and flexible application, on a case-by-case basis, of security standards to public diplomacy platforms.

Today, public diplomacy has never been more relevant or necessary to achieving U.S. foreign policy objectives and our presence in cities is vital. Foreign citizens – from civil society and religious leaders, to traditional and social media producers, to activists, to youth -- are increasingly shaping the international system. According to the National Intelligence Council's Global Trends report, increasing urbanization means that local issues can quickly become global ones. As the State Department acknowledges, diplomatic careers entail inherent risks. Diplomats must interact with state and non-state actors to do their jobs and cannot be expected to build generative networks from isolated compounds. Virtual platforms cannot replace in-person engagement, and such engagement can be very difficult to do in the face of heavy security measures.[53]

Balancing the need for foreign engagement with risk is constant and provides and an immense challenge.[54] If security conditions permit, and public engagement is in the U.S. interests, then the Secretary, along with the Chief of Mission, have the authority to issue waivers for SECCA co-location provisions.[55] We encourage these decisions to be contextual and flexible so that public diplomacy officers can more effectively carry out their mandates.

RECOMMENDATIONS

CONGRESS: Enact a "Sense of Congress" to Keep American Centers Open and IRCs Accessible.
The presumption that public diplomacy platforms should automatically be co-located within compounds, based on SECCA, should be reversed. We advise the creation of a "Sense of the Congress" in future State Department Authorization bills that clearly indicate that the Secretary of State should give favorable consideration to requests for American Centers to remain in urban locations and exercise his/her waiver authority under section 606(a)(2)(B) of the Secure Embassy Construction and Counterterrorism Act of 1999 (22 U.S.C. 4865(a)(2)(B)) in order to permit American Centers to remain separate from U.S. embassies abroad and ensure that IRCs on U.S. embassy, consulate and annex compounds remain open and accessible. This would help to simplify co-location waiver requests at the State Department and emphasize the need for a flexible, case-by-case approach that takes into consideration the centrality of public diplomacy to fulfilling U.S. missions.[58]

STATE DEPARTMENT: Aim to Make Existing IRCs Open and Accessible Through New Policy.
IRCs, especially in countries that are pivotal to U.S. national security, must become more engaging to attract audiences. A worldwide policy for open access to IRCs that applies to all posts is necessary. This would lift "by appointment only" restrictions where they exist; create a separate security screening from the main chancery; permit unescorted access; and allow use of personal electronic devices and wireless internet access. Wherever possible, U.S. employees should also have offices in the IRCs so they can regularly interact with visitors. American Centers that transform into IRCs should particularly adhere to these principles to retain relationships and networks.

STATE DEPARTMENT: Conduct a Study of the Impact of American Centers, IRCs, Binational Centers and American Corners. As a result of the 2010 Government Accountability Office (GAO) report on American Spaces, the State Department has conducted two major studies that have supported the improved management of these Spaces: a 2014 study on the user experience of American Centers and a 2015 study on the value of "by appointment only" IRCs. We also recommend a third study on the impact and value of these spaces -- American Centers, IRCs, Binational Centers and American Corners -- for U.S. foreign policy goals, especially in the IIP-determined "top tier" spaces. The appraisals should link their efforts to mission goals and develop a research-based strategic plan for each space, identifying key publics and the public diplomacy impact objectives for each key public.[59]

STATE DEPARTMENT: Continue Dialogue Between Public Diplomacy, Bureau of Overseas Building Operations and the Bureau of Diplomatic Security Leadership. We are encouraged that Diplomatic Security and the Overseas Building Operations Bureaus have already created a working group with public diplomacy leadership to address several policy, planning and funding concerns with the remaining free-standing American Centers and the IRCs. We hope that these conversations will continue to be constructive and tackle the accessibility of these spaces on a case-by-case basis.

ENDNOTES

1. U.S. Advisory Commission on Public Diplomacy. "Terrorism and Security: The Threat to Public Diplomacy." 1985. https://docs. google.com/file/d/0BzX83cntmmFqSEwt-cUg1OHFXV00/edit?pli=1; See: "Risk, Recruitment and Retention: Engaging Foreign Publics in High Threat Environments." U.S. Institute of Peace. Oct. 24, 2014. http://www.usip.org/events/risk-recruit-ment-and-retention-engaging-foreign-pub-lics-in-high-threat-environments;

2. Government Accountability Office. "Engaging Foreign Audiences: Assessment of Public Diplomacy Platforms Could Help Improve State Department Plans to Expand Engagement." July 2010. GAO-10-767.

3. A similar statement was made in support of the unique role that Peace Corps plays in U.S. diplomacy, asking for due consideration for waivers of Peace Corps volunteers. See: Statement by Congressman Christopher Shays (R-CT), May 16, 2001. Congressional Record – House 8225. http://www.gpo.gov/fdsys/pkg/CRECB-2001-pt6/pdf/CRECB-2001-pt6-Pg8212.pdf.

4. Statement by Congressman Christopher Shays (R-CT), May 16, 2001. Congressional Record – House 8225. http://www.gpo.gov/fdsys/pkg/CRECB-2001-pt6/pdf/CRECB-2001-pt6-Pg8212.pdf.

5. This recommendation was first introduced in the U.S. Advisory Commission on Public Diplomacy's September 2014 report, "Data-Driven Public Diplomacy: Progress Towards Measuring the Impact of Public Diplomacy and International Broadcasting Activities." http://www.state.gov/documents/organiza-tion/231945.pdf

6. "Secure Embassy Construction and Counter-terrorism Act of 1999." Library of Congress. https://www.govtrack.us/congress/bills/106/s679/summary

7. Office of American Spaces, Bureau of International Information Programs, U.S. Department of State.

8. U.S. Advisory Commission on Public Diplomacy. "Terrorism and Security: The Threat to Public Diplomacy." 1985. https://docs. google.com/file/d/0BzX83cntmmFqSEwtCUg-1OHFXV00/edit?pli=1

9. "The Inman Report Report of the Secretary of State's Advisory Panel on Overseas Security." U.S. Department of State. 1985. http://fas. org/irp/threat/inman/

10. Feulner, Edwin J. Jr., "Don't Let Security Hide Our Light," The Washington Post, October 7, 1985, p. A13. 5.

11. This year, the U.S. Information Agency merged with the State Department and USIA libraries became American Centers.

12. "12 FAM 440 Post security functions." U.S. Department of State Foreign Affairs Manual, Volume 12. Diplomatic Security. 16 November 2011. http://www.state.gov/documents/organi-zation/88397.pdf

13. "At posts where the terrorism or political violence threat level is elevated to critical, existing collocation waivers for U.S. diplomatic facilities are suspended pending a formal review of a new justification submittal by Post to maintain the location of the facility. Pending the review process, Posts emergency action committee must be convened to determine how quickly the facility is to be closed based on life safety issues." See: "12 FAM 440 Post security functions." U.S. Department of State Foreign Affairs Manual, Volume 12. Diplomatic Security. 16 November 2011. http://www. state.gov/documents/organization/88397.pdf

14. Foldi, Paul. "U.S. Public Diplomacy – Time to

Get Back in the Game." 13 February 2009. Committee on Foreign Relations at the U.S. Senate.

15. Ibid.

16. Ibid.

17. In addition, the report called for IRCs and American Centers to be open six days a week and to ensure accessibility, and for IRC's to be simply called "Library" as the term "Information Resource Center" often did not translate with foreign publics. In addition, the report emphasized that American Corners should not be substitutes for American Centers.

18. Government Accountability Office. "Engaging Foreign Audiences: Assessment of Public Diplomacy Platforms Could Help Improve State Department Plans to Expand Engagement." July 2010. GAO-10-767. http://www.gao.gov/products/GAO-10-767

19. Ibid.

20. Natsios, Andrew. "American Fortresses: It's Hard To Carry Out Foreign Policy From Behind Thick Concrete Walls." The Weekly Standard. 22 May 2006. http://www.weeklystandard.com/print/Content/Public/Articles/000/000/012/216yrfpx.asp?page=2. Also see: Norris, John. "How to Balance Safety and Openness for America's Diplomats." The Atlantic. November 2013.

21. "The Quadrennial Diplomacy and Development Review." U.S. Department of State. April 29, 2015. http://www.state.gov/s/dmr/qddr/

22. Ibid.

23. "2 FAM 030 Risk Management." U.S. Department of State Foreign Affairs Manual, Volume 2. General. 20 March 2015. http://www.state.gov/documents/organization/84369.pdf

24. See: "Risk, Recruitment and Retention: Engaging Foreign Publics in High Threat Environments." U.S. Institute of Peace. Oct. 24, 2014. http://www.usip.org/events/risk-recruitment-and-retention-engaging-foreign-publics-in-high-threat-environments; Wilson, Doug. "Risk, Recruitment and Retention: An All-Hands Discussion." Remarks delivered at "Risk, Recruitment and Retention: Engaging Foreign Publics in High Threat Environments" at USIP. Oct. 24, 2014. http://trumanproject.org/doctrine-blog/risk-recruitment-and-retention-an-all-hands-discussion/

25. According to the International Information Programs Bureau at the State Department, "The Office of American Spaces aims to advance U.S. foreign policy through a worldwide network of physical spaces, engaging foreign publics in interactive dialogue. The office develops and applies strategic guidance through policy and funding for these spaces to encourage person-to-person engagement. This includes providing resources to encourage the core standards of English language learning, alumni activities, cultural programs, study in the United States and information about the United States via technology. Information Resource Officers help tier one American spaces through strategic planning, oversight, and maintain access to information for visitors. The office also works with OBO and Diplomatic Security to maintain core public engagement requirements."

26. "Inspection of the Bureau of International Information Programs." U.S. Department of State and the Broadcasting Board of Governors Office of Inspector General. May 2013. https://oig.state.gov/system/files/211193.pdf

27. Office of American Spaces. International Information Programs Bureau, U.S. Department of State.

28. Ibid.

29. "2014 Comprehensive Annual Report on Public Diplomacy and International Broadcasting Activities." U.S. Advisory Commission on Public Diplomacy. Dec. 11, 1014. http://www.state.

gov/documents/organization/235159.pdf

30. Ibid.

31. "Evaluation of American Centers." Office of Policy, Planning and Resources for the Under Secretary of Public Diplomacy and Public Affairs, U.S. Department of State. 2014.

32. "Open Doors Data: Economic Impact of International Students." Institute for International Education. 2014. http://www.iie.org/Research-and-Publications/Open-Doors/Data/Economic-Impact-of-International-Students

33. Educational and Cultural Affairs Bureau, U.S. Department of State.

34. "2014 Comprehensive Annual Report on Public Diplomacy and International Broadcasting Activities."

35. Ibid.

36. Ibid.

37. See: Confucius Institute Headquarters (Habnan): http://english.hanban.org/

38. See: Goethe Institut: https://www.goethe.de/en/index.html

39. See: AllianceFrancaise: http://www.francedc.org/

40. See: British Council Annual Report: http://www.britishcouncil.org/sites/britishcouncil.uk2/files/d554_annual_report_final.pdf

41. See: Islamic Culture and Relations Organization: http://en.icro.ir/

42. See: Foldi, 2009.

43. Office of American Spaces, Bureau of International Information Programs, U.S. Department of State.

44. Note: According to the Office of American Spaces, some IRCs are considering relocating to the abandoned chanceries. These include Tashkent and Baku, although there would be more if offered the opportunity. The majority of these spaces represent urban centers that are strategically important to U.S. foreign policy goals and that most will agree face varying levels of security threats.

45. "Evaluation of 'By Appointment Only' Information Resource Centers." Office of Policy, Planning and Resources for the Under Secretary of Public Diplomacy and Public Affairs, U.S. Department of State. 2015. Notes: The Bureau of Overseas Building Operations works to identify urban areas for embassy compounds, but that is not always possible since construction must be original.

46. Ibid.

47. Ibid. Note: The evaluation found that while visitors and program participants largely understand the need for security procedures, it still acts as a deterrent. In some areas where free, ulfiltered WiFi, open access to information sources and English language learning activities are in strong demand, participants are more willing to make appointments for use of the IRC and comply with security requirements.

48. Bucharest, Romania; Lusaka, Zambia; Cotonou, Benin; Guangzhou, China; Mumbai, India; Ouagadougou, Burkino Faso; Riga, Latvia; Yaounde, Cameroon.

49. ACPD visited the Benjamin Franklin Library in Mexico City in August 2014 and asked that a co-location waiver be granted before the NEC is completed in 2020. Open since 1942, it will be uprooted from its downtown, central location in Mexico City and co-located in the NEC in an elite neighborhood in 2020. It currently advances mission goals to empower youth and entrepreneurship; protect journalists; and support science, technology, engineering and mathematics education through more than 150 annual activities, 24,000 volumes of

publications and multi-media content. It also provides English language instruction and EducationUSA advising. While the move looks inevitable, it is imperative that the new space on the NEC remain open and accessible to the Mexican public.

50. Norris, John. "How to Balance Safety and Openness for America's Diplomats." The Atlantic. November 2013.

51. See: Foldi, 2009.

52. Edwin J. Feulner, Jr., "Don't Let Security Hide Our Light," The Washington Post, October 7, 1985, p. A13. 5.

53. ACPD qualitative research has found that civilians are willing to take on more risk to complete missions important to U.S. national security, if they know they will be taken care of. See:

54. "Safer Embassies in Unsafe Spaces." March 20, 2003. Hearing Before the United States Senate Committee on Foreign Relations. http://www.gpo.gov/fdsys/pkg/CHRG-108shrg88151/html/CHRG-108shrg88151.htm

55. Government Accountability Office. "Engaging Foreign Audiences: Assessment of Public Diplomacy Platforms Could Help Improve State Department Plans to Expand Engagement." July 2010. GAO-10-767.

56. Government Accountability Office. "Engaging Foreign Audiences: Assessment of Public Diplomacy Platforms Could Help Improve State Department Plans to Expand Engagement." July 2010. GAO-10-767.

57. A similar statement was made in support of the unique role that Peace Corps plays in U.S. diplomacy, asking for due consideration for waivers of Peace Corps volunteers. See: Statement by Congressman Christopher Shays (R-CT), May 16, 2001. Congressional Record – House 8225. http://www.gpo.gov/fdsys/pkg/CRECB-2001-pt6/pdf/CRECB-2001-pt6-Pg8212.pdf.

58. Statement by Congressman Christopher Shays (R-CT), May 16, 2001. Congressional Record – House 8225. http://www.gpo.gov/fdsys/pkg/CRECB-2001-pt6/pdf/CRECB-2001-pt6-Pg8212.pdf.

59. This recommendation was first introduced in the U.S. Advisory Commission on Public Diplomacy's September 2014 report, "Data-Driven Public Diplomacy: Progress Towards Measuring the Impact of Public Diplomacy and International Broadcasting Activities." http://www.state.gov/documents/organization/231945.pdf

60. Cabral, Roxanne; Peter Engelke, Katherine Brown, Anne Wedner. "Diplomacy for a Diffuse World." Atlantic Council & U.S. Advisory Commission on Public Diplomacy. September 2014. http://www.atlanticcouncil.org/images/publications/Diplomacy_for_a_Diffuse_World.pdf

61. "Safer Embassies in Unsafe Spaces." March 20, 2003. Hearing Before the United States Senate Committee on Foreign Relations. http://www.gpo.gov/fdsys/pkg/CHRG-108shrg88151/html/CHRG-108shrg88151.htm

ADDENDUM

TOP TIER AMERICAN SPACES

Africa

Pretoria, South Africa - American Corner Pretoria
Bulawayo, Zimbabwe - W.E.B. DuBois American Center
Kigali, Rwanda - Kigali American Corner
Kinshasa, Democratic Republic of Congo – American Corner Limete
Addis Ababa, Ethiopia -- Addis Ababa American Corner
Kisumu, Kenya – American Corner Kisumu
Lagos, Nigeria - AfriLabs Lagos
Thies, Senegal – American Corner Thies
Cape Town, South Africa -- USinfo@Central

East Asia Pacific

Rangoon, Burma – American Center
Mandalay, Burma – Jefferson Center
Chengdu, China - Chengdu Information Resource Center
Shanghai, China - Shanghai American Center
Shenyang, China - Shenyang Information Resource Center
Beijing, China - Beijing American Center
Jakarta, Indonesia - @america
Seoul, Korea - American Center Korea
Hanoi, Vietnam – American Center
Ho Chi Minh City, Vietnam - American Center Ho Chi Minh City

Europe

Mostar, Bosnia & Herzegovina - American Corner Mostar
Batumi, Georgia - Batumi American Corner
Stuttgart, Germany - German-American Institute
Xanthi, Greece - Xanthi American Corner
Chisinau, Moldova - American Resource Center Chisinau
Lisbon, Portugal - Faculty of Science and Technology
Moscow, Russia – American Center Moscow (really an American Corner)
Gaziantep, Turkey - Gaziantep American Corner
Kyiv, Ukraine - Kyiv America House
Kharkiv, Ukraine - Kharkiv Window on America Center

Near East Asia Region

Cairo, Egypt - IRC Cairo
Cairo, Egypt - American Corner Maadi
Amman, Jordan - American Language Center
Baakline, Lebanon - American Corner Baakleen
Casablanca, Morocco - Dar America
West Jerusalem, Israel - American Center Jerusalem
East Jerusalem, Palestinian Territories - America House Jerusalem
Ramallah, Palestinian Territories - America House Ramallah
Tunis, Tunisia – American Corner Tunisia
Aden, Yemen – American Corner at Aden University

South and Central Asia

Dhaka, Bangladesh - Edward M. Kennedy Center
New Delhi, India - The American Center New Delhi
Kandy, Sri Lanka - Kandy American Corner
Malyy, Maldives - American Corner Malyy
Kathmandu, Nepal - Nepal Book Bus
Karachi, Pakistan – Lincoln Learning Center
Almaty, Kazakhstan - American Corner Almaty
Bishkek, Kyrgyz Republic - Bishkek America Borboru
Dushanbe, Tajikistan - Dushanbe American Corner
Ashgabat, Turkmenistan - IRC Ashgabat

Western Hemisphere Affairs

Argentina, Buenos Aires - Instituto Cultural Argentino Norteamericano
Cochabamba, Bolivia - Centro Boliviano Americano Cochabamba
Brasilia, Brazil - Casa Thomas Jefferson
Santiago, Chile - Instituto Chileno Norteamericano
Pereira, Colombia - Centro Colombo Americano
Cuenca, Ecuador - Centro Ecuatoriano Norteamericano Abraham Lincoln
San Pedro Sula, Honduras - Centro Cultural Sampedrano
Mexico, Mexico City - Benjamin Franklin Library
Managua, Nicaragua - Centro Cultural Nicaraguense Norteamericano
Maracaibo, Venezuela - Centro Venezolano Americano del Zulia

Page Intentionally Left Blank

Page Intentionally Left Blank